Series editor
ALISTAIR
BRYCE-CLEGG

fantastic ideas for
engaging dads

FEATHERSTONE

FEATHERSTONE

Bloomsbury Publishing Plc

50 Bedford Square, London, WC1B 3DP, UK

BLOOMSBURY, FEATHERSTONE and the Feather logo are trademarks of Bloomsbury Publishing Plc

First published in Great Britain 2018 by Bloomsbury Publishing Plc

A catalogue record for this book is available from the British Library

ISBN: PB: 978-1-4729-4984-4; ePDF: 978-1-4729-4985-1

2 4 6 8 10 9 7 5 3 1

Printed and bound in India by Replika Press Pvt. Ltd.

To find out more about our authors and books visit www.bloomsbury.com and sign up for our newsletters

Contents

Introduction

Whether they are part of a relationship or a single-parent family, dads matter. Research shows that their influence makes a positive difference to children at every stage of development.

Did you know that men have a physical, hormonal response to becoming fathers? These hormones, including oxytocin, oestrogen, prolactin and glucocorticoids, create a natural protectiveness towards their baby, and levels of these hormones increase the more they hold their newborn babies, creating an even stronger bond. Sensitive, affectionate and supportive involvement from dads in the month following the birth onwards leads to a range of positive outcomes in babies and toddlers. These include improved cognitive, social and language development, better performance and ability to face challenges and frustrations at school, stronger psychological wellbeing and lower levels of delinquency (Rosenberg et al., 2006).

Dads enrich children's skills and knowledge by broadening their horizons and increasing their interest in a wider range of activities. Whether it's film or cars, books or football, dads' personal interests present children with opportunities to extend their language and engage in deeper conversations. Dads play differently to other caregivers and, generally, they are more comfortable with engaging children in risky play.

It is universally agreed that the frequency of dads reading to children is associated with better emergent literacy outcomes and a greater interest in books later in life. Dads singing a lullaby, telling a story or repeating funny rhymes enrich children's experience not least because of the different intonation, accents and speech sounds.

Dads also help children become young mathematicians. Dads who take note of their children's interests and build on them provide a strong starting point to support and extend their mathematical thinking. For girls, having a supportive dad has been linked to them having more confidence with maths.

Our purpose with this book is to make you aware of these important findings and to provide activities so you can create a bridge between the home and the nursery. Of course, children also benefit from other men in the family taking a supportive interest in their learning. Granddads can bring additional benefits to children, and the role of boys and men in the family such as uncles, big brothers and cousins can enrich a child's learning opportunities even further.

The activities in this book can be done in the nursery as a trial run so that when sharing the ideas, staff have tested and refined them for their particular group. You can share these ideas with dads on a parent notice board, send them home on home learning sheets or just discuss them in casual child development conversations.

Rosenberg, J. & Wilcox, W. B. (2006). *The Importance of Fathers in the Healthy Development of Children*. USA: Office on Child Abuse and Neglect, U.S. Children's Bureau.

The structure of the book

The purpose of this book is to help you recognise the importance of encouraging dads to get involved at every level of their child's development. The book provides a range of activities which can be used both in the nursery and at home. We recognise that many dads may have limited time and energy, so this book is designed to support staff to show dads how simple actions – whether it be the routine bedtime story or a 'dads in the nursery day' – can make a big difference to their child's potential. Before you start any activity, read through everything on the page so you are familiar with the whole activity and what you might need to plan in advance.

What you need lists the resources required for the activity. These are likely to be readily available in most settings and homes or can be bought/made easily.

What to do offers step-by-step instructions for practitioners and dads.

The **Health & Safety** tips are often obvious, but safety can't be overstressed. In many cases, there are no specific hazards involved in completing the activity, and your usual health and safety measures should be enough. In others, there are particular issues to be noted and addressed.

What's in it for the children? tells you briefly how the suggested activities contribute to learning.

The **Taking it forward** section helps you consider what else you can do to extend the learning experiences. It gives ideas for additional activities on the same theme, or for developing the activity further.

Finally, **Advice for dads** offers guidance for making the activity successful and safe.

Ball and spoon

What you need:

- A large space, indoors or outdoors
- A spoon each
- A ball each that will fit on the spoon

What to do:

1. Clear a space where you can't break anything.
2. Give a spoon and ball to each child.
3. Ask the children to stand still while the dads put the ball on the spoon.
4. The children should start with small movements, moving with the spoon a little way until some confidence is gained.
5. Once ready, the children should walk steadily across the space.
6. To increase the learning, encourage them to walk faster and slower, and hold the spoon at different levels.
7. When the children are confident walking with the ball and spoon, ask them to swap the spoon into their non-dominant hand.

What's in it for the children?

Children will develop their balance and spatial awareness skills through this play. This activity will also encourage the children to concentrate for a stretch of time on one activity. Holding the spoon in the palmar grasp will be the most efficient way of balancing the spoon, and it's good practice to get them used to holding things in this way.

Taking it forward

- Different types and sizes of spoons and balls will offer different levels of challenge.
- A traditional ball and spoon race can be a great way to encourage dads into the setting.

Advice for dads

The children probably won't be very good at this activity at the start!

Den building

What you need:

- Paper
- Coloured pens and pencils
- Pieces of fabric, towels, sheets, tablecloths
- String
- Tape
- Pegs
- Cushions or pillows
- Camera

What's in it for the children?

Designing and building a structure requires planning and foresight. The children will develop their physical coordination while working on their problem-solving skills. Problem solvers need to develop: attention skills, concentration, perseverance and confidence to succeed.

Taking it forward

- Outside dens could be built from old branches, crates, pallets, off cuts of wood, large planters, etc.

- Once the den is built, dads and children can sit and read together and enjoy their new space.

Advice for dads

Creating a den, nook or corner to play, read or draw in at home is a great way to give your child some independence. Cosy nooks are perfect for naptime too!

What to do:

1. Talk to the children about what makes a perfect den. Encourage them to be creative in their thinking.

2. Give the drawing equipment to the children and ask them to draw their ideal den based on your discussion.

3. Allow the children to start building their dens using any soft materials you have available. What else can they find to add to their den? A den can be built anywhere: under a table, with two chairs together, behind the sofa or outside in between two large items. Ensure any structures built are secure and safe.

4. When building their den, suggest they check the plans against the emerging edifice. Encourage them to consider whether they need to alter their plans.

5. Dads should aid and cooperate with the children, but respect the master architect's final decisions about what the den should look like!

6. Photograph the building process and make a simple book documenting the stages to completion. Invite the children to choose one of their teddies, superheroes or special things to turn their den into a little nurture nook.

Rough and tumble

What you need:

- Lots of energy
- An outdoor space free from hazards, sharp corners and furniture
- Rugs
- Cushions

What to do:

1. Clear a space, preferably outdoors, so that it is free of hazards. Scatter rugs, cushions and other soft furnishings to create a softer landing environment.
2. Start from a low crouching position or lying down to limit hard knocks and falls.
3. Dads should use their body to bounce, rock and roll with their child.
4. Encourage the child to pause and think of their next move.
5. Chat about the fact that dads are stronger and bigger than children.
6. Dads should sometimes let the child lead and help them discover new ideas and ways of moving.

What's in it for the children?

Children will develop gross motor control and body strength while play fighting with dads and each other. The challenge of staying upright will help to improve their coordination and cultivate their sense of bravery. An understanding of give and take and an awareness of body language and how to read it are all important in developing children's social skills.

Taking it forward

- Introduce some clear, competitive objectives to the play, e.g. children must get past the dads to reach a certain goal.

Advice for dads

Don't be scared – this seemingly simple activity is much undervalued.

I spy

What you need:

- Kitchen timer
- Binoculars (either real of made from cardboard rolls)
- Magnifying glass
- Miragescope

What's in it for the children?

Playing 'I spy' is a great way to develop children's vocabulary and challenge them to apply knowledge they have in a different way. It helps the children become more observant by examining their environment and the many objects within it. The game also demands a high level of listening and concentration, and allows them to demonstrate understanding of descriptive words.

Taking it forward

- Playing 'I spy' in unfamiliar settings can introduce further challenge.

- Big and complicated words are actually fascinating for children. 'Chandelier' or 'candelabra' are not any harder than 'diplodocus' or 'pterodactyl'!

Advice for dads

Start with easy items and then increase the level of difficulty.

What to do:

1. Introduce the rules of the game. Set a time limit, either using a kitchen timer or by counting to ten.

2. Use the first letter or the first sound of the word. If known, using the Makaton sign for the letter can help children to catch on quicker.

3. You can help the child by pointing towards the object or giving a clue.

4. You don't have to play the 'I spy' game with initial sounds, especially if the child is not at that stage in their literacy learning. Instead, you could give a clue, e.g. 'we have one of these in the sitting room hanging from the ceiling' (light) or 'we eat these after dinner they are small and red and round' (cherries).

5. Allow the child to use the binoculars, magnifying glass or miragescope to focus their attention on searching for the item you have named.

6. Once the child has successfully guessed the answer, reaffirm their response by touching or pointing to the object and repeating its name.

Minibeast hunt

What you need:

- Explorer costumes and hats (optional)
- Magnifying glass
- Torch
- An outdoor space where insects may be living
- Paper
- Coloured pens and pencils

What to do:

1. Dress up in role-play costumes to create a sense of wonder and excitement by pretending to be great explorers.

2. Take the magnify glass and torch and look in the dark places of a park or garden.

3. Describe the insects as you find them.

4. Listen carefully to see if they make a sound.

5. Later, do some further research and ask the children to draw the insects you found.

6. Make a minibeast diary with the child's drawings and write descriptions. Dads can scribe for the children.

What's in it for the children?

Exploring the world is a great way to promote scientific curiosity. Searching for minibeasts will develop children's fine motor skills and their observation skills. There will be a lot of new vocabulary associated with an activity like this one.

Taking it forward

- Look in a book of common garden insects before you set off and see if you can find your favourites while you are exploring.

- Watch the insects for a short while and see if you can make up a story about them. Perhaps the little woodlouse is being naughty and the big woodlouse is telling him off.

Advice for dads

There Was an Old Woman Who Swallowed a Fly is a great poem to read after the activity to keep the discussion going.

Frame it

What you need:

- Two photo frames with the glass removed
- Smartphone

What to do:

1. Taking turns, go around the setting and identify something the child likes. It could be anything from sprouting broccoli, their favourite flower or the first letter of their name/superhero/favourite toy.

2. Put the frame around the object to provoke a conversation. It's great fun to do at the table. Frame the piece of cutlery that the child thinks they will use first or the most to eat lunch.

3. Frame things at the supermarket. Challenge them to find something green to frame or a fruit or vegetable they don't know the name of and so on.

4. Photograph anything that elicits a strong response using your smartphone so you can continue the discussion later if you like.

What's in it for the children?

This activity will develop their awareness of their surroundings. Leading the children in purposeful conversation and asking them to make choices about what to frame will improve their exploration skills.

Taking it forward

- Rather than seeking an object to frame, ask the child to create a composition on a theme, e.g. their favourite blue things, things they found in the garden, and so on. Frame and photograph it – now you have a piece of art, without any of the mess of paint!

Advice for dads

Make sure you take turns and encourage conversation to extend the child's thoughts.

Wishes to blow

What you need:

- Freshly-picked dandelion seed heads (alternatively: feathers, small petals, leaves or bits of potpourri, crêpe paper shreds)
- A folded paper fan

What to do:

1. Look closely at the dandelions seed heads together.

2. Talk about the different parts of the plant and why it looks the way it does. Decide whether it's a 'weed' or a 'flower'.

3. Ask the children to tap the flowers gently to see what happens. Dads should describe what is happening.

4. Have a chat about wishes, hopes and dreams. Tell the children about the hopes and dreams you had when you were small – perhaps you wanted to fly like a bird, be a superhero or climb the tallest mountain.

5. Use the paper fan or your breath to blow the 'wishes' into the sky.

6. If you can't find the dandelion seed heads, then use some of the other suggested items to create a similar experience to share.

What's in it for the children?

Playing with nature in this way offers an easy introduction to the life cycle of a plant. There is also a strong element of understanding the world in this play because the children are exploring cause and effect, movement, and flight.

Taking it forward

- Use the fan on yourself to 'blow' your hair at the front and sides. Do it to the children so they can feel the breeze.

Advice for dads

This is a great opportunity to give the child a space to blow away things that are worrying them.

Nature walk

What you need:

- An outdoor space such as a field, garden, woodland or beach where you might easily and safely find different leaves, petals, sticks, stones, grasses, twigs and shells
- A basket, small bag or box

What's in it for the children?

Interacting with nature and creating from nature will nurture an appreciation of it and all its colours, textures and shapes. Children can observe the minute differences in every leaf, stick or branch they collect. Getting outdoors can help develop children's gross motor skills through reaching, stretching and gathering. They will also develop their fine motor skills through the manipulation, placing and inspection of the objects found.

Taking it forward

- If the children collect items from the floor such as a leaf, ask them to locate the plant it originated from. Discuss differences between the fallen leaf and the living one.
- Use the items you collected to create a picture, pattern or piece of art.
- While the children are creating their pictures, encourage them to chat about their ideas. Once they have finished, ask them to tell the 'story' of their creations.

Advice for dads

Make a frame for their outdoor art with some twigs and sticks.

What to do:

1. Take the children on a walk togethe. Bring a basket to collect leaves, petals, sticks, stones – whatever interests the children.

2. You might set a target such as 'can you find ten items'. Increase the challenge by setting a more specific target, e.g. find four round things and two long ones.

3. As you walk, talk about what you find. Encourage the children not just to name the found items but also to say something about them, e.g. 'oh this leaf is damp and a bit floppy'.

4. Each time you select something to add to the collection, use interesting and challenging words. Reaffirm words the children know and introduce new words.

Blackboard painting

What you need:

- Small blackboards, or cardboard covered in blackboard paint
- A clipboard or plastic tray
- Chalks
- Flour or icing sugar
- Spoons
- Flour sifters
- Cotton buds
- Small tub of water

What's in it for the children?

The children will investigate the properties of materials. They will examine and observe how things change when they interact with other things. This activity will encourage the development of gross and fine motor skills.

Taking it forward

- Make handprints in the flour using two hands. Compare the size of dads' hands with children's.
- Use big paintbrushes, feathers, etc. to create patterns and marks on the floured/chalk surfaces.

Advice for dads

Don't worry about making a mess – a good vacuum cleaner will collect any powder that spills.

Health & Safety

Make sure children do not inhale the powders and be aware of allergies before you start.

What to do:

1. Invite the children to join you on the floor, at a table or in the garden.

2. Present the blackboard and tell the children you are going to create art using chalk and/or flour. Ensure the blackboard is stable on a clipboard or tray before you start; upright blackboards must be securely fastened to the wall.

3. Demonstrate how you can create a chalk paste by dipping the chalk in water before using it. Let the children explore making marks with dry and wet chalk.

4. Introduce the flour or icing sugar and explain the importance of not inhaling these.

5. Encourage the children to gently cover the blackboard in a thin layer of the flour/chalk using spoons, flour sifters and their hands.

6. Offer them a cotton bud; they should wet the cotton bud in the water and use it to draw on the blackboard. Dads should join in on the same blackboard or place their own blackboard next to their child's.

Conker creativity

What you need:

- Conkers
- Leaves
- Twigs
- Shells
- Nuts
- Stones

What to do:

1. Collect a selection of natural items from around the setting and outdoors. Invite the children to make a pattern with the objects.

2. Ask the children to display all of the natural objects in a designated space.

3. Don't set any expectations for them or tell them your ideas; let them come up with something on their own.

4. While they explore independently, dads should sit with the children and talk about what they are doing. They should use positional language, e.g. 'in front of', 'behind', 'next to', to describe the children's display. Children should be encouraged to use positional language themselves if they feel confident.

5. Dads could choose to create a little spiral of their own alongside the children.

6. Remind children that it's also okay to be quiet; silence can sometimes be better than lots of chat that interrupts their thinking.

What's in it for the children?

Developing an understanding of position and using positional language is important for mathematical development. In this activity, children can explore natural objects, their relation to one another and patterns.

Taking it forward

- Focus on developing descriptive language, describing the texture or positions and patterns being created.

- Can the children place all the items in a line and then a circle or create a sequence with them?

Advice for dads

Encourage your child to change their creations using the materials again and again. The essence of this activity is that it is NOT permanent.

Make a bird feeder

What you need:

- Shredded suet
- Wild bird seed
- Weighing scales
- Saucepan
- Wooden spoon
- Any leftover sunflower seeds, stale cake crumbs, cheese crumbs or seeds from dock, thistle knapweed, teasel or ragwort
- A small tin (washed and dried) or a coconut shell

What's in it for the children?

The children will learn about wildlife, in particular local birds and animals. Working together to cook a meal (even for a bird) demonstrates to children the importance of care giving and looking after the environment. The children will learn more about number and measurement, as well as new vocabulary such as the names of birds.

Taking it forward

- Encourage the children to keep an observation diary, and take photos of the birds feeding.

- Over time, allow the children to experiment with which 'extras' the birds in your area prefer.

Advice for dads

Don't use salted nuts, desiccated coconut, highly-spiced food or very dry bread as these are all bad for birds. Check out the RSPB website for free information about birds, including games, videos and recordings of bird calls.

What to do:

1. Ask the children to weigh out 100 g of suet and put it in a saucepan. Dads should help the children to melt it over a gentle heat.

2. The children should then weigh out 100 g of seed, adding in any extra ingredients they wish to include from the selection provided. One part suet, one part seed and extras will produce a good mix.

3. When the suet is liquid, turn off the heat. Dads should remove the pan from the cooker, and allow the children to stir in the seeds and other ingredients. The mixture should look quite sticky as this is what holds it together once cool.

4. Leave the mixture to cool slightly.

5. Ask the children to tip the mixture into the tin or coconut shell. Leave to cool and set completely.

6. When it is set, dads should help children to string up the tin or shell, or wedge it into the branch of a tree in an outdoor space where the children will easily be able to see birds visiting it. Be sure to hang the feeder in a position where the birds can eat safely without being attacked by cats or foxes!

Come in, come in, over...

What you need:

- Two empty, clean yogurt pots or plastic cups
- A drawing pin
- A pen
- String

What's in it for the children?

Children will begin to think about and understand that sound is a vibration that travels through string and other media. They will develop their focus and concentration when speaking to watch and see the vibrations on the string – they're not visible to the naked eye, but they can try!

Taking it forward

- Try the 'chat' from in front of a door and behind a door, leaving it slightly ajar.
- Allow the children to hypothesise and experiment: what happens when the string goes round a corner? Does it still work? What happens when you make the line longer or really long?
- Investigate what kind of voice works best – a whisper? Do we have to use a loud voice? Or does it work best with our normal voice?
- Is it important to keep the string from touching something, i.e. the ground or table top?

Advice for dads

Don't worry that it doesn't seem to be loud and clear. Remember it's just illustrating how sound travels.

What to do:

1. Help the children to make a hole in the bottom of each of the yogurt pots or plastic cups using a drawing pin.
2. Use the pen to make the hole bigger.
3. Thread the end of the string though one of the holes.
4. Tie a large knot to stop the string falling back through. The knot should be 'in' the yoghurt pot, not on the bottom. Repeat with the other pot.
5. Your communicator/telephone is now ready to use!
6. Invite the children to hold one of the pots to their ear.
7. Then, standing as far away from them as your string will allow, speak into the other cup. Can they hear you? Ask them to touch the string as you speak 'down the line'.
8. Explain that when you talk into the pot or cup, the string picks up the vibrations that are generated by your voice and transmits them along its length. On arrival at the other end of the string, the sound is then heard (broadcast) in the other pot!

Real tool play

What you need:

- A few toy tools and real tools such as a hammer, saw and pliers
- Safety goggles
- Tacks or nails
- Pieces of soft wood
- Pieces of cork

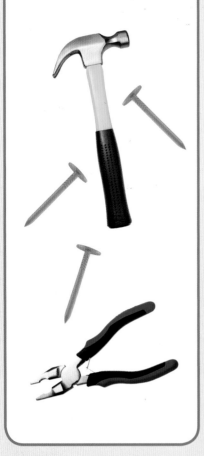

What to do:

1. There are many conflicting views and opinions about using real tools with young children. Perhaps the best 'measure' is how you feel about it. If children sense that you are nervous, that may hold them back or make them hesitant.

2. Discuss the tools – what they are made of and what they are for. Invite the children to handle them carefully while wearing safety goggles. Emphasise the importance of treating tools with respect and why it's important to take care of them.

3. Demonstrate how to use the tools. As you do this, ensure they are watching and concentrating. Highlight the appropriate and safe way to use them and the dangers of misuse.

4. Allow the children to give the tools a try. Again, explain the need to be careful, slow and considered when using the tools.

5. Show the children how to hammer a nail into the wood and cork and how to pull it out again with the pliers. Encourage them to practise using the techniques you have demonstrated before working together to create something specific.

✚ **Health & Safety**
It is very important that children are highly supervised; this activity should be done in partnership, together.

What's in it for the children?

Children will learn how to use tools and try techniques in a safe and appropriate way. This activity will help them overcome apprehension and develop confidence and delight.

They will expand their creative thinking by using their maths and scientific investigations skills, as well as developing their coordination, grasp and manipulation skills.

Taking it forward

- Plan with the children where they may want to place bottle tops before they attach them to the wood with a hammer and nail.

- Set a specific challenge such as to create a face, a spiral for a snail shell or the letter at the start of their name.

Advice for dads

Start with a small project you can work on together.

Creating a wood model

What you need:

- Some balsa wood – consider the weight and thickness
- Paper
- Pencils
- Measuring tape
- Ruler
- Child-sized saw, if available
- Adult saw
- Safety goggles
- Nail tacks
- Hammer
- Wood glue
- Thick corrugated cardboard

What's in it for the children?

The children will develop an idea of size and measurement. They will practise their fine motor skills while using their small muscles to manipulate the various tools and pieces of wood.

Taking it forward

- Decorate the finished objects with pens, glitter glue and washi tape.

Advice for dads

Use the tools for short moments and build up to actually sawing or nailing.

 Health & Safety

It is very important that children are highly supervised; this activity should be done in partnership, together.

What to do:

1. Put out a variety of shapes and sizes of the wood pieces.
2. Talk to the children about the wood; compare the pieces by weight, size and shape.
3. Ask the children to use the paper and pencils to design an object to create. This might be a bed for their doll or a car for their teddy, for example.
4. Discuss construction and measurements with the children; decide how large the pieces of wood need to be. Help the children to mark the wood with pencil along the cutting line.
5. Introduce the tools. Invite the children to handle them carefully while wearing safety goggles. Emphasise the importance of safety, and demonstrate how to hold the tools appropriately and safely.
6. Allow the children to saw through the lines they marked earlier.
7. If dads are not comfortable or are concerned with their child's ability to use the tools, they could opt to do most of the sawing while the children place their hand on top of the dad's hand. Remind them to be brave but safe!
8. Construct the object using nail tacks, a hammer and wood glue. Use corrugated cardboard for lighter structures such as roofs of houses.

Tin tin

What you need:

- Empty tin cans of various sizes and depths
- Sandpaper
- Brushes
- Magnetic paint
- Small items that may or may not be magnetic such as small world toys

What's in it for the children?

Investigating magnetism through play can ignite children's curiosity about the world around them. They will learn about predicting the outcomes of their experiments and about cause and effect.

Taking it forward

- Use the cans to play a game of 'tin can alley'. Place the cans apart from each other and take turns to try and knock them over with a ball. Then place them so the magnetic paint makes it a little more challenging.

Advice for dads

Make sure the children wear aprons to paint. Check the paint for caution notices and pay attention to the fumes and instructions about safety on the labels. Do not assume you know.

What to do:

1. Gather a range of tin cans; discuss the importance of recycling with the children. Dads should sand the rough edges along the rims of the cans as they are collected.

2. Allow the children to explore the cans – what sounds do they make when bashed together? Can the children stack them? Can they fit inside one another? How many are there?

3. Offer the children a brush each. Encourage them to coat the tin cans with the magnetic paint. Cover some surfaces and not others.

4. Once dry, allow the children to play with the cans once again. Use the cans themselves to create magnetic structures, or use some small world toys to climb on, over and in the structures.

5. Gather small items from around the nursery or home and ask the children to guess how magnetic they are. Stick them to the cans and experiment!

Dad builds a mud kitchen

What you need:

- Bowls (or an old kitchen sink, if you can get one!)
- Kitchen utensils such as:
  - Saucepan
  - Potato masher
  - Sieve
  - Whisk
  - Garlic press
  - Pestle and mortar
  - Wooden juicer
  - Honey dipper
  - Turkey baster
- Mud

What's in it for the children?

As the children role play and use the various utensils, they will develop both fine and gross motor skills. They will use a range of big movements as they transfer mud between bowls and surfaces. As they create their concoctions, they will develop their concentration skills.

Taking it forward

- Create 'clean mud' as an alternative: shred or finely rip some paper, then grate some soap into the mixture. Pour warm water over it and stir. The mixture, when manipulated by hand or spoon, will be like lumpy mud!

Advice for dads

The messier the better!

What to do:

1. Gather a few bowls, kitchen utensils and mud.
2. Set the items out so the children have easy access to them.
3. Ensure there is plenty of room so the children can mix, 'cook' and create potions and lotions.
4. Encourage the children to pour, whisk, stir and create lots of marvellous mud concoctions.
5. As they use each of the utensils, dads should name the item and discuss what happens when they are used in the mud.
6. Suggest the children name the 'dishes' they create.

Make a magic fairy garden

What you need:

- Access to a park or woodland to gather materials including:
  - Pebbles and stones
  - Bark and twigs
  - Leaves and plants
- Tyre
- Small pot plants
- Small world figures
- Small plastic animals

What's in it for the children?

Such activities offer a good provocation for imagination. Children will gain confidence and understanding of nature and the outside world. They will develop their gross motor skills by exploring the park or woodland for suitable materials.

Taking it forward

- Arrange to visit the fairy garden on a sunny day and read fairy books with the children.

- Sing to the garden to encourage fairies to visit!

- Encourage the children to visit the fairy garden and whisper their wishes to the fairies.

Advice for dads

Don't worry about the children getting dirty. Let the children lead, just nudge their ideas forward. Encourage them to be as fantastical in their play as possible, and don't be shy of doing the same.

What to do:

1. Discuss fairies in general and ask the children for their favourite fairy stories.

2. Go on a nature walk in the park, woodland or gardens to find items for the magic garden.

3. Gather pebbles, stones, bark, twigs, leaves and anything else that might be useful. Encourage the children to choose special items that they think the fairies will like, including their favourite small world figures.

4. If possible, place a tyre on the ground to create the magic garden space. If not, create an enclosed safe space such as at the bottom of a tree or under a bush.

5. Choose a few small pot plants or annuals such as violas, pansies or cyclamen. Engage the children in designing the fairy garden. Dads should help by planting any living plants and decorating the fairy garden with their child.

Scavenger hunt

What you need:

- Printed scavenger hunt list, one for each child
- Pen or pencil
- A small prize
- Bag or basket
- Whistle or timer
- Camera (optional)

What to do:

1. Prepare the scavenger hunt lists in advance. Good topics for the children to hunt include: colours of the rainbow, shapes, something beginning with each letter of the alphabet, and so on.

2. Create some excitement as the children are told of their task to make it more thrilling. Tell the children about the prize for the fastest hunter.

3. Allocate the tasks. If dads each take one child, then it's simpler. If dads have more than one child each, then allocate different tasks to different children.

4. Be clear about the task. Ask the children to locate the item and put it in their bag or basket.

5. Depending on the age and stage of the children, the scavenger hunt lists could be a list of photos for the children to tick off or a written list for the dads and children to read out together.

6. Use a whistle or a timer to start and stop the activity.

7. Dads could take photos of the children as they collect the items to prove that there was no cheating!

8. Give a prize to the team who were fastest to find all of the items on their list.

What's in it for the children?

Working together as a pair or part of group will require children to listen carefully, follow instructions and work cooperatively. A scavenger hunt can work well anywhere. It's great for getting groups, families or just a few children out and about. The park, the local shopping centre, the garden or the walk to nursery are all excellent options.

Taking it forward

- Scavenger hunts can be repeated again and again. Each time, children will find different evidence! Include more imaginative tasks such as a seeking a magic number door or discovering a new shape.

- Help them to manage their fears in a safe way using this play. If they are afraid of the dark, try a scavenger hunt at dusk and provide children with torches.

Advice for dads

This is different from a treasure hunt because you don't have to spend ages making clues. Just ask the children to find items that already exist in your environment.

50 fantastic ideas for engaging dads

Scissor success

What to do:

1. Introduce the scissors and discuss how they work.

2. Point out that they can be dangerous so the rule is that you should never run with a scissors, and you should point the scissors downwards when moving about.

3. Identify the benefits of a short snip versus a long cut.

4. Ask the children to describe the paper using words and ask them to guess how difficult different types of paper will be to cut.

5. Establish the difficulties of cutting each thickness through experimentation.

6. Encourage the children to cut a variety of shapes based on the worksheet. Can they create any shapes of their own?

7. Talk about any difficulties they encountered, such as cutting on a curve.

What's in it for the children?

The children will develop their fine motor skills and use of the palmar and pincer grasps. They will be challenged to use their concentration and determination.

Taking it forward

- Make a collage from the shapes the children have cut out.

- Discuss the importance of recycling the left-over paper.

Advice for dads

Scissors should be sharp enough to cut with a little pressure; scissors do more damage if they are blunt.

Making a fishing rod

What you need:

- Fishing line
- Sturdy stick, 4 to 5 feet long
- Scissors
- Fish hook
- Plastic bobber
- Bait

What's in it for the children?

Fishing is a great way to practise concentration and patience. Dads can learn about the good care of fish and good fishing practices alongside their children through books and videos. Children will need to practise speaking quietly but clearly so as not to scare the fish.

Taking it forward

- Visit the local fishing shop with the children and talk to the staff there.
- Read a storybook about fishing.
- Read a non-fiction book about fish and discuss which fish you are likely to find in your area.

Advice for dads

The best type of stick for your fishing rod is strong, yet slightly flexible. Bamboo, about one half-inch thick, would be ideal.

✚ Health & Safety

It is very important that children are highly supervised; this activity should be done in partnership, together. Count the number of hooks used and make sure you get the same number back.

What to do:

1. Dads will need to help the children construct the fishing rod.

2. Tie one end of the fishing line to the thicker end of the stick – this will be the handle.

3. Wrap the line in a spiral around the stick until you reach the tip. Tie the line firmly to the tip, but don't cut the line just yet.

4. Unroll the line about a foot longer than the stick, and cut it off the roll. You should have a continuous length of fishing line extending from the handle of your stick down to the hook. (That way, if the fishing rod breaks in the middle, you still have the line in your hand.)

5. Tie a hook to the end of the line.

6. Fasten a bobber to the middle of the line. You'll want to use a ball-shaped red and white bobber with a spring-loaded hook that will fasten it anywhere on the line.

7. Now you're ready to fish! For bait, use worms.

Tell me a story

What you need:

- A comfy, cosy space
- Quiet
- An idea for a story or an old favourite
- Any props related to your story

What to do:

1. Dads should start their story with familiar opening lines such as 'once upon a time' or 'one day…' so the children know what is coming.

2. Try to introduce a new word and then weave it into the story a few times so the children remember it and can make sense of it within the context of the story.

3. Dads could use an experience that happened earlier in the day, tell an old favourite from their own childhood or come up with something truly fantastical of their own.

What's in it for the children?

There is a long tradition of oral storytelling in many cultures as this is one way of bonding and sharing experiences. Stories expose children to new words and make them practise listening carefully in order to follow the story. Expressive storytelling can help children learn to read facial expressions. Children will also start to anticipate what will happen next, understand the structure of a story (beginning, middle and end) and connect elements of the story to their own life.

Taking it forward

- Take it in turns to narrate a story – you never know where you might end up!

Advice for dads

Don't always think you need a book to tell a story. Try and weave the child's name into the story and some other familiar points of reference.

Read me a story, Dad!

What you need:

- A favourite story book

What's in it for the children?

Reading with children is a vital part of allowing them to become book lovers. Parents can be tempted to read the story through and ask a few questions at the end, but often don't take time to let the child look at and imagine the story or context in which it's set. The approach to reading set out here will help their confidence grow, their attention and concentration develop and focus their thinking on more than just the words.

Taking it forward

- Dads can use household items and create a story together with their children. Place the items in an order on the floor and 'weave' an oral story.

- Dads could scribe the story the children create and draw some pictures together to illustrate it.

Advice for dads

Make sure you find a quiet, cosy place with no phone, television or noisy interruptions.

What to do:

1. Remember that children first 'read' a book by looking at the pictures and illustrations. Talking about what they see rather than worrying about the words is often the best starting place.

2. Dads should use a dialogic reading approach. This means they should prompt the children to respond to the content during the reading session.

3. Draw the children's attention to an illustration and say 'oh look'. This will prompt the child to say something about the book.

4. When they name a character or say something about the illustration, such as 'cow', evaluate their remark by repeating 'yes, a cow' or 'oh, a cow'.

5. Expand on the comment by saying 'yes, it's a cow, a big cow' or 'a black and white cow' or 'a cow who is eating the grass'. Don't just use basic words such as big and small – think 'massive', 'gigantic', 'enormous'. If there are flowers in the picture, don't just call them flowers – use 'daisies', 'tulips', 'gerberas' (even if it's not clear what flowers are in the illustration).

6. Repeat the prompt to ensure the child has listened or so they can have another go at commenting on the illustrations.

7. It's very supportive to consider fully the illustrations and let the child really explore what the pictures say. They often have much more detail than the words.

Techie dad

What you need:

- Smartphone or camera
- Photos
- Tablet computer
- A story book
- Music

What to do:

1. Take some photos on a walk together. As you walk, talk about what you are seeing and taking photos of.

2. When back home, look at the photos and ask the child to recall in which order you saw the photographed objects or where you saw them.

3. Take photos of the items you are buying in a shop. Once home, show the child the picture of each item and ask them to find it in the shopping bags.

4. When reading a story with the children, use the tablet to look up some of the real things in the story. For example, if there is a castle in the story, have a look at some castles. If the story has houses in it, such as in *The Three Little Pigs*, then look at some houses from around the world and discuss how different they all are.

5. Record some short clips of music with different beats and rhythms then dance together.

6. Don't just use technology as a 'babysitter'.

What's in it for the children?

The children will develop an understanding of what is going on with technology today and this will help them in their later lives. Dads can demonstrate how to use technology and explore the purpose of each of the different pieces of equipment. Dads should show how useful technology can be to extend an idea or explore an image.

Taking it forward

- Dads and children could go on a tech hunt. In each room in the house or setting, identify things that need to be plugged in, use electricity, are portable, or change when switched on. Identify the technology and talk about how we use it in our daily lives.

Advice for dads

There is lots of research on the use of technology with young children. It would be an idea to consider how often and for how long you offer access to any tech – it's best to introduce it in small doses and it's not great for those under two. When sharing it with your little ones, be sure to give it purpose.

Counting dad

What you need:

- A good repertoire of number rhymes
- Anything can be counted such as teddy bears, building blocks or food

What's in it for the children?

Very young children will start to count spontaneously and later begin to refine their skills by pointing their finger at the objects they are counting. They often try to get all the numbers they know in their count as they pass their finger along the objects. They also reuse numbers – they have not finished and they have used up all their known numbers, so they will begin using the same numbers again. Regular practice is the most important thing for number development.

Taking it forward

- Make little number cards and place them around the house or setting. If there are four toothbrushes put a numeral '4' up beside them. Six mugs on the rack? Place a numeral '6' nearby. On the stairs, number them up from zero.

Advice for dads

Stimulate children's enthusiasm to learn new numbers. Don't worry about them getting the numbers in the right order or the 'perfect' counting sequences. Larger numbers fascinate some children (often boys); they often talk about '100' or '1000' and know that it's a 'big' number.

What to do:

1. Ensure you know the chosen number rhyme off by heart before you begin teaching the children, or use a book of number rhymes. Old favourites such as 'Five little speckled frogs', 'One, two, three, four, five' and 'Ten in a bed' are perfect for young children, and dads might even remember them from their own childhood.

2. Introduce rhymes systematically, so that children can increase their repertoire of favourite rhymes. Ensure you practise the songs regularly so the children learn them off by heart.

3. Use the props to practise counting with the children as you sing the rhymes.

4. When a child points to each object individually and they count and match a tag (a number) to each object, they are counting – even if the numbers aren't quite right. Count along with them.

Racing dad

What you need:

- A variety of cars – small, large, heavy, light
- A selection of other wheeled toys
- Paper
- Paint

What to do:

1. Place all the wheeled toys on the floor or flat surface.
2. Invite the children to explore how they move. Do you need to push them? If you pull them back, do they rush forward?
3. Play a racing game with the cars.
4. Place the paper along the surface.
5. Dip the car wheels into paint and then run them on the paper to create track prints.
6. Once dry, look at the wheels on each vehicle and try to match the track print with the vehicles that made them.

What's in it for the children?

The children will develop an idea of speed, energy and forces. They can explore cause and effect as they push and pull the cars. This activity can be a first step towards mark making, and offers an idea of direction as they create a 'map' of the journey.

Taking it forward

- Go on a walk and spot the different vehicles that have wheels and tyres on them. If you safely pass near some that are parked, have a look at the patterns on the treads.

Advice for dads

Go for speed – crashes are the order of the day!

Slinky play

What you need:

- Slinkies – as many as you can get, in a variety of colours and materials

What to do:

1. Let the children explore the slinkies first.

2. Introduce the words that describe the movement as it occurs such as 'stretch', 'squash', 'wiggle', 'bend' or 'swing'.

3. Encourage the children to stretch them out. Children may be reluctant to stretch them out at first in case they retract and snap their fingers.

4. Stretch them and weave them onto each other. Attach them to create larger slinkies.

5. Set some challenges, like balancing them on alternate hands.

6. Show the children the slinkies 'walking' down the stairs.

7. Have a slinky race. Dads and children should compete to see whose slinky gets to the bottom of the staircase fastest.

What's in it for the children?

Children will be able to observe the effects of energy, forces and friction in action, though they do not yet understand them fully. They will practise their physical skills and, in particular, small and large manipulative movements. This activity can also develop their reaction times and encourage them to be brave when approaching potential hazards.

Taking it forward

- Stretch out one of the slinkies and secure it to a tree with string or ribbon. Weave materials through the spirals. Peg some pieces of paper or material onto the slinkies to create 'rooms'.

Advice for dads

This activity is all about getting your child to be brave and take a chance on extending the slinky as far as possible without panicking about the consequences.

Building a house

What you need:

- *Three Little Pigs* storybook
- Straw (or drinking straws, in case of allergies)
- Sticks and twigs
- Blocks – shop bought or homemade
- Abrasive sponges
- Velcro rollers
- Sticky tape
- Pegs
- Measurement tape
- Spirit level
- Scarfs or tea towels
- Cardboard

What to do:

1. Read the story of the *Three Little Pigs* to introduce the idea of houses made from different materials.
2. Gather a range of materials that the children could build with.
3. Initially, set out the straw, sticks and 'bricks' and ask the children to recreate the story. Ask them to talk about what they are doing as they play.
4. Introduce the extra materials.
5. Suggest you make a house for their toys and teddies. They could make towers, walls or an enclosure. Encourage the children to 'measure' their buildings and use the spirit level to check it (dads will need to help with this).
6. Use a scarf or towel to create the roof if the children can't make a structure strong enough to hold a cardboard roof.

What's in it for the children?

This activity is great for improving children's fine motor skills, but the real challenge is using problem-solving skills to design a structure from unusual items that are neither smooth nor even, rather than the more traditional blocks or bricks.

Taking it forward

- Encourage the children to draw a plan before they start building, or to stop and rethink the plan by drawing the changes they want to make.

Advice for dads

Look at the different structures people have lived in across time and around the world. They all look so different so use this to stimulate the planning stage or to create weird and wonderful structures.

Block tower

What you need:

- **A variety of blocks, Duplo®, stickle bricks or Lego®**
- **Sticky tape**
- **Sticky tack**

What to do:

1. Place whatever blocks you have onto the floor.

2. Place the sticky tape and tack beside the blocks.

3. Challenge the children to create a structure. Suggest that they can use the sticky tape and sticky tack if they need to.

4. You could put in an additional challenge by asking the children to only use a certain number of blocks. Make sure to count the blocks with the children as they use them.

5. Ask the children to make a tower at least a metre high or up to their dad's knee.

What's in it for the children?

Block play is important to develop children's physical skills. It promotes the pincer, tripod and palmer grasp – all necessary for when the children are ready to write. Children will develop an understanding of balance and have to practise being patient when the blocks fall down. If dads count the blocks as the children build, this will increase their awareness of number.

Taking it forward

- Put a time limit on the activity. Challenge the children to build the highest tower possible in 20 seconds.

- Ask the children to predict how high it will be in 30 seconds. If they are to build the longest line of blocks, how far do they predict they will reach in 40 seconds?

Advice for dads

Don't always tidy up right after a build – leave it for a little while as your child may like to revisit and add to the build.

Discount shopper

What you need:

- Paper
- Pencils
- Local discount shop
- Couple of pounds

What to do:

1. Plan the shopping trip with the children beforehand. Dads and children should make their own shopping lists. The children's shopping lists won't necessarily be legible!
2. Let the children take the lead.
3. Walk around the shop.
4. Talk about what they see.
5. Talk about what they like and dislike.
6. Ask the children to name their favourite items. Decide which of their favourite items they can afford from the amount of money available.
7. Dads should help the children pay for the items chosen.
8. Remind the children to say 'please' and 'thank you'.

What's in it for the children?

The children will extend their language and learn new transactional vocabulary. They will learn how shopping works and about the expected behaviour in a shop. Experiences like these are important to build their confidence in communicating. Understanding the value of goods and money is a valuable early experience. Children will enjoy the walk which is good for their all-round health.

Taking it forward

- Set a shopping challenge. Suggest you collect three fresh items and then see if you can find an alternative in a jar or a can. What about in the frozen section? This will offer the children a broader understanding of the various ways food is packaged.

Advice for dads

See the extraordinary in the ordinary. Look at the unusual shapes and textures of the fresh fruit or the smells and scents of the flowers.

What will we wear today?

What you need:

- Pictures of people in different weather conditions
- A variety of clothes for different kinds of weather

What to do:

1. Look at the pictures of people in different weather conditions. Discuss how many of them the child has actually experienced themselves.
2. Gather the clothes. You could do this beforehand or with the child.
3. Sort through the clothes and name each item as you examine it.
4. Sort the clothes into piles by colour, size, type of garment, etc. Let the children lead the sort.
5. Suggest you look outside and see what the weather is doing. Ask the children to sort a pile of clothes for that kind of weather. What if it was snowing, would they need to wear something different?

What's in it for the children?

This will help the children develop observation skills and invite them to offer suggestions and opinions too. They will develop sorting and categorizing skills while improving their awareness of weather conditions that mean they have to choose appropriate clothing.

Taking it forward

- Do a dress up relay race. Place a couple of items in a few places round the room – some for summer, some for winter. One person should say a type of weather and then it's a race to find four items for that type of weather and put them on!

Advice for dads

This is a great opportunity for your child to practise learning to dress themselves, a skill that is much appreciated when they go to school.

Through a telescope

What you need:

- Old newspapers to protect your tables
- Three colours of paints
- Plastic or paper plate
- Three cardboard tubes
- Paintbrushes
- Scissors
- Sticky tape
- String
- Stickers
- Felt tip pens

What's in it for the children?

This is a simple activity that helps children practise their fine motor skills as they paint and decorate the tubes and work out how to make them tight enough to slide inside each other. It encourages much conversation and more opportunities to practise learning about colours and size.

Taking it forward

- The telescope can be made longer and include more complicated decorations.
- Talk to the children about how we use telescopes. Ask them to guess how they work.
- Visit an observatory with the children to learn more about telescopes.

Advice for dads

How about doing this activity before the pirate hunt on (p.47)?

What to do:

1. Spread the newspaper on the table to protect it.
2. Put the three different paints on a plastic or paper plate in separate blobs to make it easy to manage.
3. Paint the cardboard tubes in the three different colours. Let them dry.
4. Dads should cut a line right down the middle of one of the tubes and roll it tighter so it slips inside one of the other tubes.
5. Ensure the narrow roll can slide in and out of the larger one and then secure it with sticky tape.
6. Do this again with the final tube. Make sure this one fits inside the tube you have already cut.
7. Cut two lengths of string about 18 cm each.
8. Feed the string into the smallest tube and secure at the top with sticky tape
9. Feed the string through the medium tube and then through the largest tube. Secure the string to the inside of the largest tube with sticky tape.
10. Decorate the telescope with the stickers and felt tip pens.

Making a mandala

What you need:

- Mandala templates
- Paints
- Paintbrushes
- Coloured pens and pencils

What to do:

1. Download, print or buy some mandala templates.

2. Depending on the age and stage of your children, offer a range of quite simple symmetric shapes and more complicated diagrams.

3. Dads and children should choose a design together and select their colouring materials from the selection available.

4. Discuss colour and pattern. Challenge the children to think of a different pattern for each section of the mandala (e.g. stripes, polka dots, zig zags).

What's in it for the children?

This activity offers the children a chance for some quiet time concentrating on painting or decorating. This is an opportunity for dads and children to work together on something creative, with no expectations about what they will produce. Dads should help the children to develop and extend their language of shape, space and colour.

Taking it forward

- Print the mandala on large paper and allow all of the children to work on the same one.

- Use découpage techniques to decorate and upcycle an old table or stool. This is a great opportunity to talk about sustainability too.

- Link the activity to mindfulness strategies, such as meditations and music.

Advice for dads

To begin, keep the shape simple. It's a new activity and best to start in an uncomplicated way.

Making a paper aeroplane

What you need:

- A piece of paper

What to do:

1. Fold your paper in half lengthwise making a good strong crease and unfold.

2. With the paper in a portrait orientation in front of you, fold both of the top corners down to the middle crease to make a basic 'house' shape (a square with a triangle on the top).

3. Fold the slanted edges down toward the middle crease.

4. Fold the right side over to the left side along the middle crease you made in step 1. Make sure that all your folds are on the inside.

5. Fold the left edge back on itself to form a wing.

6. Turn the paper over and repeat to make a wing.

7. Unfold the wings upwards slightly.

8. Fly!

What's in it for the children?

This activity requires focus, determination and fine manipulation skills. The fine motor skills developed in this activity will help the children when they are ready to write. The children will indirectly learn about forces and gravity.

Taking it forward

- Decorate the paper before making the aeroplane.

- Use different kinds of paper such as origami paper, cardboard and newspaper.

- Have a competition to see who can fly their aeroplane the furthest.

Advice for dads

Don't get cross if your aeroplane won't fly!

We're going on a letter hunt

What you need:

- Coloured pencils
- Paper
- Cardboard binoculars
- Frames from old glasses
- An old picture frame
- Create some frames with cardboard different sizes

What's in it for the children?

A firm grasp of letter recognition is essential to prepare children for reading. Through this activity, children will learn that reading is about recognising words in all different places, not just in a book. It also gives the children the opportunity to practise the letter sound and shape in a more natural way by spotting it in their environment and naming it.

Taking it forward

- Take a photo of each letter you find and then make a collage of the photos later.
- For older children, give them a clue e.g. 'this animal has a long, fluffy tail and says "meow"'. They need to solve the clue to know the letter. Then, they need to find the letter in the room to win.

Advice for dads

This is great fun if it's not forced and you stick to a few letters.

What to do:

1. Choose a letter from the alphabet.
2. Draw the letter a few times in different sizes and colours on the paper and discuss with the children where you have seen it recently. Look in magazines, on a ketchup bottle or food can, or on a poster in your neighbourhood.
3. Suggest you go and hunt for more.
4. Put a little collection of tools for searching together such as cardboard binoculars, old glasses or an old picture frame to capture the letter when you see it. It gives the activity a touch of excitement.

Pirate Dad's treasure hunt

What you need:

- Pirate 'treasure', e.g. gold chocolate coins, small trinkets
- Paper
- Old teabags
- Tally sheet and pen

What to do:

1. Prepare in advance five to ten items of treasure for the children to find. Hide them around the setting, garden or space.

2. Create a treasure map made from paper stained yellow from cold teabags. It doesn't need to be perfect, but make sure you include some 'landmarks' so the children can orientate themselves.

3. Give each child a treasure map.

4. Invite the children into the space and tell them that there are five to ten items of treasure buried or hidden around them. Give them a special card to make tally marks as they collect the treasure.

5. You could also ask the children to mark on their map where they found the treasure, then return to their dad for a treat once they have found them all.

What's in it for the children?

By counting off the 'treasures', children will develop their numeracy skills. They will need to understand the concept of distance, time and measure in order to navigate using the map. If the children work with the dads or each other to locate the treasure, they will develop valuable communication and compromise skills.

Taking it forward

- Do a tissue paper treasure hunt. Gather a few small objects that the children are familiar with. Wrap them in tissue and place them around the room. Tell them you have hidden some treasure and let them find it. Give the children the list of objects; challenge them to identify the treasure from the size and shape of the tissue wrap. Once they have guessed, they can open the parcels to see if they were correct.

Advice for dads

Be aware of the maths concepts your child has developed. Ensure your expectations are not too high.

Number hunt

What you need:

- Coins
- Newspapers
- A clock
- Mobile phone
- Watch (digital and analogue)
- Oven clock
- Weighing scales

What to do:

1. The aim is to introduce numbers to the children in a natural and fun way in their immediate environment.

2. Explore the numerals on the coins, newspapers, a clock, mobile phone, watches, front of the oven, weighing scales, etc.

3. Suggest you look around the house or setting for more numbers.

4. Then go on a number hunt outside!

5. To make it fun, set a target to find certain numbers. Dads and children should compete to find the most numbers.

6. If you meet anyone on your walk, ask them about numbers. How old are they? What is their date of birth? What is the number on their front door?

What's in it for the children?

The children will develop their understanding of number and number names, as well as where numbers are used and what they are used for. Early number exploration is about building the children's confidence in identifying and naming numerals, ready for learning number sequences.

Taking it forward

- Spontaneously choose a number and then have a look around to see if you can find examples in the immediate environment.

- Each time you find one of the numbers, count them or tally them on a piece of paper.

- Invite the children to predict which number will occur most frequently.

Advice for dads

Counting is best learned if it's repeated throughout the day and in natural situations. Try to get into the habit of counting out loud when paying for things or setting the dinner table.

Door colour challenge

What you need:

- Paint colour sheets from the DIY store
- Clipboard or notebook
- A pen

What to do:

1. This activity will introduce new colours, reinforce existing knowledge and explore shades of colour.

2. Before you set out, say to the children that you are thinking of painting your front door. When people come to visit, they may get it mixed up because all the doors are the same – or are they?

3. Give each child a set of colour sheets on a clipboard or stuck into a notebook.

4. Go for a walk in your neighbourhood.

5. Ask the children to put a tick next to each colour as you find it.

6. At the end of the walk, count how many ticks each colour has. Tell the children you would like an unusual colour that not many people have. Ask them to tell you what colour they think you should paint your door.

What's in it for the children?

Colour is part of mathematics; learning, recognising and understanding tones and hues of colour is very important. Searching for colours develops children's observation skills, and by introducing colour tones and hues, this activity offers good language extension. The children will practise their counting skills at the end of the session. They will need to evaluate their data to decide the best colour.

Taking it forward

- Extend this activity to cars, coats, bags, etc.
- If the child knows most colours, introduce shades such as lime, turquoise, bottle green, etc.

Advice for dads

When in a street, be aware of traffic and road dangers. Have a chat about road safety before going out.

Measure the puddle

What you need:

- Puddles
- Your feet
- Welly boots
- Sandals or flip flops

What to do:

1. Choose a rainy day for this activity so there are lots of natural puddles around. May or June are the best times of year – warm, wet summer showers are perfect.

2. Ask the children to select some of the footwear and explore the puddles with the dads. Talk about the sensation of the water on toes, or through the boots.

3. What happens when we jump and make an impact on the water?

4. What makes the water splash or burst out from under our feet/shoes?

5. What if it's a muddy puddle, do we squelch?

6. Suggest they estimate how many 'feet' (their own feet) wide the puddles are.

7. The children should measure the puddles with the dads by placing one foot directly in front of the other. Discuss how the children's feet and dads' feet differ in size. Dads should offer help with balance (if necessary) and support with counting. Who can find the biggest puddle?

What's in it for the children?

The children will develop an understanding of cause and effect and how water reacts to force – if they stomp in the puddle, water will splash out. They will practise their measuring skills, with dads offering physical and intellectual support in case they get stuck.

Taking it forward

- If there are enough puddles, try to get the children to splash in time with a nursery rhyme such as 'Doctor Foster'.

- Record the sound of the children splashing and play it back.

Advice for dads

Be prepared for your child to get wet!

Paintball

What you need:

- Old clothing
- Large sheets of paper (old wallpaper or newspaper would work)
- Stones
- A selection of balls, different sizes, shapes and textures
- Different paint colours
- A paint tray

What's in it for the children?

The children will explore different movement and materials in this activity. They will be given the opportunity to mark make in an unusual way and develop their gross motor skills. When fully engaged with this activity, it can help children to develop their upper body and shoulder pivots.

Taking it forward

- Use teabags to 'splat' the paint rather than rolling it. Take a used teabag, dip it in paint then drop or gently throw this at the paper.

- Move the paper further away and 'target' each throw to a different part of the paper for additional challenge.

Advice for dads

Be prepared to get messy and sticky!

What to do:

1. Find suitable space outside to make a mess. Ensure dads and children are wearing old clothing.

2. Dads and children should spread out the paper on the ground and secure the corners with stones.

3. Encourage the children to explore the different balls through dropping, rolling, bouncing, pushing and spinning them.

4. Pour the paint onto a tray and suggest the balls are dipped in the paint and then used to create a little 'story' on the paper.

5. Dads could take photos as the picture appears and encourage the children to describe what the patterns look like.

6. Dads and children could sit opposite each other and gently roll the 'dipped' balls to each other or softly bounce the ball to each other.

7. Dads could place a dipped ball each at one end and lift the paper to make the paint covered ball 'run' along the paper.

Tape it up

What you need:

- A book or newspaper with lots of photos of buildings
- Cardboard boxes of various sizes
- A roll of woodchip paper or any old ends of wallpaper
- Sticky tape, duct tape or gaffer tape (brightly coloured or patterned, if you can)
- Coloured pens and paints

What to do:

1. Look at buildings and towers in a book or newspaper, or on the internet. Walk around the area if you can and see what kinds of buildings are near you. Talk about the scale of the buildings.

2. The idea is to create a set of large 'bricks'. Find anything with a cuboid shape and cover it with wallpaper.

3. Children can help dads to achieve this or dads could surprise them by having prepared the pile of bricks in advance.

4. Encourage the children to decorate the blocks with the coloured tapes or with pens and paint.

5. Once the blocks are dry, ask the children to build lots of different structures. Can they balance a few 'bricks' on top of two of their structures? What about a long wall?

6. Challenge them to use ten bricks in three different ways. Suggest that the children challenge the dads too.

7. Invite the children to stand the bricks on their thin edges against each other. Can they create a triangle with the floor as the third side?

8. Could they use the 'bricks' to create a house shape?

9. Could they guess how high they can build with the bricks before they topple?

10. If you have a pile of sponges or cushions, the children can create towers and topple them over again and again.

What's in it for the children?

The children will develop an idea of materials and how they feel, move and can be used. The blocks offer excellent opportunities to build on their counting, building, balancing and sorting skills. They can also help the children to understand height and perspective.

Taking it forward

- This is a good basis for introducing games such as Jenga® and other building games that extend the children's balance and dexterity.

Advice for dads

Make sure you have lots of space for this activity.

Mirror, mirror

What you need:

- Set of pattern blocks for each child
- Mirrors

What to do:

1. Give each child a set of pattern blocks and a small mirror.

2. Ask children to create a design with their blocks and name the shape or colour as they place each block.

3. Then have them hold the mirror up to each side of the design to see how it appears to be flipped in the mirror.

4. Examine other objects around the setting using the mirror, e.g. the clock is a still circle but the numbers are backwards in the mirror. The door is still a rectangle, but the handle is on the wrong side in the mirror.

What's in it for the children?

Children will use shape vocabulary to describe the pattern blocks and the shapes they create using them. Dads can extend children's vocabulary and introduce positional and relational vocabulary. This activity can help develop early understanding of mirrors, though it will be some time before children fully appreciate how they work.

Taking it forward

- Use multiple mirrors and explore how they reflect each other.

- Introduce some unusual mirrors such as a magnifying mirror or a wavy mirror.

Advice for dads

Clear the area and background so the reflections 'pop'.

Dads do soup

What you need:

- A simple soup recipe
- Antibacterial spray
- Chopping boards
- Vegetables
- Water
- Knives
- Saucepan
- Stock
- Wooden spoon

What to do:

1. Find a simple soup recipe and explain the process of what you are going to do with the children.

2. Clean down any work surfaces using antibacterial spray and set out the chopping boards.

3. Line up the ingredients along the table so the children can name and describe each item.

4. Dads should read out the recipe and children should collect the correct quantity of each vegetable.

5. Children should wash their vegetables.

6. Model how to use the knives safely and allow the children to begin chopping. Dads should offer close support and may need to pre-chop the sturdier vegetables before the children can have a go.

7. Ask the children to put the chopped vegetables in the saucepan with some stock.

8. Dads can help the children to cook and stir the soup.

What's in it for the children?

Cooking is an early science; the children will learn about how things change with heat. They will also learn about weight and measures, and the cooking conversation will enhance their vocabulary. This activity is a good opportunity to talk about where food comes from and the different foods we eat.

Taking it forward

- Take the children shopping for the vegetables before starting the activity.

- Create regular cooking opportunities and enhance your repertoire with smoothies, biscuits, scones and cakes. Perhaps pick some blackberries and make jam.

Advice for dads

Encourage your child to be actively involved; don't just let them watch you cook.

Peg it race

What you need:

- A length of rope, string, ribbon
- A range of clothes, towels, face cloths, washing cloths, pillow cases, socks, etc.
- Lots of pegs in a range of sizes (many craft shops have tiny pegs)
- Dice
- A timer

What's in it for the children?

Pegs are an excellent (and cheap) resource to develop children's fine motors skills and pincer and tripod grips. Using the pegs can be quite challenging for younger children, so dads should be on hand to assist when needed. The children will need to puzzle out how best to hang their items so they don't fall off the line – some will be heavier, some lighter.

Taking it forward

- Introduce a competitive element by challenging the children to peg faster than their dads.
- Suggest that you could create patterns with the pegs. For example, small, big, small, big or blue, red, yellow, blue, red, yellow, and so on.

Advice for dads

Only use dirty washing – it's likely the clothes will end up on the floor at some point!

What to do:

1. Set up an outdoor or indoor space so there is a 'washing line' at an appropriate height for the children.

2. Explain that you always find pegging up fiddly and a bit difficult. What you would like to do is get better at it, so you have decided to see how well and quickly you can do it.

3. Suggest that dads and children each take a few items of clothing and some pegs. Children should count as they hang them up.

4. Invite the children to roll the dice. The number on the dice is the number of items they have to hang! Challenge them to see how quickly they can hang them using a timer.

5. Do the activity first with larger pegs, then suggest you try with the smaller ones. Is it harder or easier?

6. You could then reverse the race: time how long it takes to 'unhang' the 'washing'.

7. Chat about which pegs would be best for which piece of fabric. Are the small pegs easier to use than the big ones?

A letter for someone special

What you need:

- Paper (plain printer paper for drafting and special paper for letters)
- Card
- A range of pens and pencils
- Envelopes

What's in it for the children?

'Writing' in this way will strengthen children's palmer and pincer control, important for more formal writing. They will need to use their small muscles, and hand-eye coordination. Dads will help the children to understand the concept of writing a letter and what happens when you post it. This offers a great introduction to another form of communication, and children will hear new words in a new context.

Taking it forward

- Visit the person who received the letter so the children can better understand how letters and post work.
- Dads could add a little note in the child's letter to the recipient asking for a response. Children will love the anticipation and excitement associated with receiving letters as well as sending them.

Advice for dads

Using technology to communicate is great but it limits the manipulation of your child's fine motor skills. Drawing and writing on a daily basis is fabulous for life skills and is an easy way to see something completed.

What to do:

1. Gather a variety of paper and some envelopes.
2. Choose some pens and pencils. If possible, put them in a box or wrap them in a piece of fabric to make them more special. An old briefcase from a charity shop would be ideal.
3. Dads should to practise writing some letters and writing shapes such as curves, dots and lines.
4. Invite the children to 'help' the dads.
5. Dads should explain that they are going to write a letter to a friend or relative and suggest the children write one too.
6. Chat about what they might write and draw.
7. Remember it doesn't matter what the writing looks like or whether it makes sense; this is for fun! It's a great opportunity to reaffirm all the teaching you have been doing on letters.
8. If you can, walk to the post office and actually post it.

Making gloop

What you need:

- Bowls
- Jugs
- Cornflour
- Water
- A few different sized spoons

What to do:

1. Set the bowls and jugs next to each other.
2. Suggest that you will become scientists and take turns to lead the experiment. Before you begin, discuss what you will do with the 'ingredients' for your experiment.
3. Spoon some of the cornflour into the bowl, then pour some water in. Ask the children to mix and stir it with the spoon.
4. Invite the children to use their hands to make sure it's all mashed together. We have made a compound!
5. Repeat the experiment with different quantities of each ingredient and compare the mixtures. Which smells the best? Are any thicker or runnier? Ensure the children do most of the work but dads should help and support. Some of the compounds are harder to stir.

What's in it for the children?

This is really a game of patience, awe and wonder. The children will see how things change when mixed together. They will develop an understanding of liquids, solids and compounds. There is also an element of decision making to this activity; children will explore how their decisions on quantity affect the outcome of the experiment.

Taking it forward

- Add some more special ingredients such as food colouring, flavour extracts or glitter for a greater sensory experience.

Advice for dads

This is messy so make sure old clothes are worn and do it outside or not near a carpet.

Dinosaur swamp

What you need:

- Lots of natural items such as grass, twigs, stones, leaves, moss, etc.
- A space to play outside in a garden area (or a large bowl, tuff tray or box)
- Gloop (see p.62 with blue or green food colouring)
- Dinosaurs toys (or your hands with a face drawn on)

What to do:

1. Before the activity, go on a nature walk with the children to gather natural items such as grass, twigs, etc.
2. Build a swamp with the children using the collected materials. Add some coloured gloop.
3. Put the dinosaurs in the swamp.
4. Give one of them a name and voice, e.g. 'This is Stego. He has a really loud, rough voice'.
5. Invite the children to name the other dinosaur toys and create personalities for them.

What's in it for the children?

This activity encourages children to go outside and play with the elements that we find in our natural world. Dads can help to build their children's vocabulary of nature. Children's imaginations are much better than adults for imagining things. We may assume too often that children need props and toys to stimulate their imaginations but often they prefer to pretend. This sort of play can encourage and extend their imagination and communication as they make the dinosaurs talk to each other in the swamp.

Taking it forward

- Build a more permanent swamp structure outside if there is space. This could be an old plastic box or a tuff tray.
- Introduce sand and other materials for additional sensory elements.

Advice for dads

Don't be afraid to really get into character.

Dads come to nursery

What you need:

- Invitations to your event
- Coloured pens and pencils
- Glitter glue
- Dads (or significant male role models)

What's in it for the children?

Children will be very pleased and will receive a boost to their confidence; they will love showing their dads around the nursery and engaging them in their favourite activities. Children will also learn that not everyone has a dad living with them. Some dads may not be able to attend, but we can use this opportunity to teach the children resilience and how to manage their disappointment.

Taking it forward

- Hold regular dad days where dads can pop in and play with the children.
- Visit some dads in their workplace – if one dad is a shopkeeper, visit his shop; if another is a train driver, visit the train station.

Advice for dads

If you can't attend for whatever reason, invite other men who matter to your child.

What to do:

1. Print some basic invitations with the details of the visit; this might be for a specific activity, for breakfast or lunch or for a fundraising activity. The possibilities are endless. Get it right so it suits your dads and they will come.

2. Ask the children to decorate the invitations using the resources available.

3. Encourage the children to give them to their dads or the most significant male role model in their lives (this may be an older brother, uncle or grandad).

4. When the dads arrive at the setting for the event, follow your usual routine. Ask the children to show their dads how to hang up their coats nicely and how to take the register.